EVERYONE'S DAUGHTER

Everyone's Daughter

Marguerite Floyd

WIND PUBLICATIONS

 For information address Wind Publications, 600 Overbrook Drive, Nicholasville KY 40356

International Standard Book Number 978-1-893239-91-3
Library of Congress Control Number 2009932609

First edition

Acknowledgements

Some of the poems in this volume previously appeared in *ACE Magazine, Bellows, Cincinnati Poetry Review, Cold Mountain Review, Eleventh Muse, Fabbro, Kentucky Poetry Review, Live Oak Review, Moon, Moondance, Wind,* and *Town Meeting.*

Front cover photo by Scott Liddell, www.scottliddell.net

I owe much to many in the cause of poetry,

but most especially to

James Baker Hall and Jack Myers.

Contents

part one

picture book 3
new year's morning 4
leaving 5
dishes 6
darkroom 7
astronomer 8
skipping stones 9
secret work 10
inventory 11
silent sister 12
ferryman 14
limestone 15
tell me 16
ghost 18
october 19
chocolate 20
phases of the moon 21
evening meal 23
perspective 24

part two

t.s. eliot is dead 27
ironweeds 29
every night 30
dusk 31
absence 32
gravity 33
final circle 34
feeder 35
counting 36

wishbone	37
they will tell lies at your funeral	38
turning	39
bodies	40
salt	42
saying goodbye	43
begetting	44
mechanics	46
widow walk	47
usual story	48

part three

lines	53
pattern	54
quilts	55
this house	56
cold country	57
brilliance	58
for a piano player	59
chameleon	60
tourist	61
sunflowers	62
bridges	64
hallways	65
fourth of july run	66
crescent moon	68
yoga	69
witness	70
high dive	71
road work	72
i don’t care	74
everybody’s daughter	75
crossing the divide	76
about the author	79

I

THE PICTURE BOOK

In the piano bench my grandmother kept
a picture book of a woman with no arms.
Every time I found it she denied any memory
of where it came from, how it came to be
in her parlor, tangled amid the sheet music.

The woman did everything with her feet.
On one page she stirred dinner and
I would study her developed toes
as they grasped the spoon, trying to imagine her
lifting a fork to her lips. I couldn't even manage
to practice the scales with my ten fingers
still intact. Further on she held her smiling
children with her legs, her husband beaming
over them all with a smile only the happy know.
Between the pictures the text explained
the power of faith in big type.

If it had been thirty years later she could have
told her story on cassette, sold the rights
to a big inspirational outfit, maybe even hosted her
own television show. She was pretty enough.
A happy, well-adjusted all-American woman without arms.
I couldn't imagine her ever crying the way my mother cried.

It could happen to me, I knew. Already I understood
I would never outgrow the immensity of life's accidents.
And then who would love me, without arms, without hands?
And then what would happen to me?

NEW YEAR'S MORNING

The grass was glazed with ice,
The still green blades breaking underfoot
Like the bones of small animals.
With a little effort one might have combed
That grass, parting the blades
From the flakes of snow and ice, might have
Smoothed it back into some semblance of spring,
A premature birth to portend a willingness to begin again.

The dream being done I put on my coat to leave
And found a circle of children, a family
Playing kickball, heads bowed as though in prayer
With the solemnity of priests bearing sacraments.

Ignorant of priests and children I stood beyond
Their circle, as if being offered other choices,
Choices requiring a faith I had not yet learned,
The faith of snow falling on warmer ground.

Heedless of me the children played on,
Their hands pocketed against the day's cold,
While the broken barn braced itself with ice
And the earth waited for a far-off thawing.

LEAVING

All through the long loneliness
of the Pennsylvania interstates
I thought I was returning
to myself, thought I was escaping
you like some accident
missed by five minutes. All night
the trucks passed me indifferently, their tires
scarring tracks in the rain I tried to follow
as if we were all headed for the same place.

I made lists in my head of what I would do
when I had safely arrived,
clicked them off like a grocery list;
the necessary coffee, the marmalade
you never cared for. I promised myself
sleep, hours of unbroken rest, days
of nothing but solid healing.

I always reach the mountains at night.
I doubt now they even exist in sunlight,
only loom like the black shapes
of someone else's nightmares.

Now I awaken at three a.m. to sirens crying
out like voices promising help. I untangle
the sheets and wonder what error
of judgement has called forth the forces
of the city in such alarm.

How long before I make the same fatal error?
Or have I made it already, the act of leaving
so large and dark no siren will find me,
no one hurry to lift me from the wreckage?

DISHES

Sometimes all I can do is wash dishes,
go through the house gathering up
ashtrays and forgotten glasses,
washing things clean and putting
them out again.

If I wanted clarity I could do the windows.
If it was order I craved there are closets
to be emptied. The laundry needs
to be done again and I should
get the bills in the mail.

But there are things in my life so large
that all I can see is the clutter
we're leaving along the way.

Last night we circled and circled
the same questions until the
dawn bled its light into the sky
and we saw nothing
was any clearer, nothing
had been settled and put away.

From my kitchen window this morning
I see my neighbor step from her house,
carrying her briefcase to the car.
She drives off into the depths
of the city, trailing confidence behind her
like leaves scattering in her wake.

DARK ROOM

There are days when all I want
is to pull the blinds and sit
in dark rooms. Maybe turn on
the radio and not listen
to any of the songs.

Any room would do
as long as it kept out the sun
and allowed me to unplug the phone
so no one could call to say
I've been disconnected.

I'd put a cool cloth
over my eyes and lie back,
forgetting the pavement shimmering
like the long slow waves
of the open sea miles beyond
the littered shoreline.

I've let too many things go
their own random way.
Their jangling as they crowd
for their places gives me
a headache nothing
but darkness will cure.

If I had a dark room
I'd close my eyes and
let my face develop
into someone else's.

THE ASTRONOMER

She knows the constellations
girdling the night, knows
which pinprick of light
buckles the belt of Orion,
which gleam bares
the wheat in Virgo's hand.

In every season she charts
stellar motion in a dance
of mathematics, Polaris as zero
holding, like the eye of God
immutable and fixed.

This is what she's always trusted
the heavens so large and sure
there can never be any error,
any uncertainty of her place amid
the milky tangle of stars.

As she works
the Earth is resettling itself
against the Sun, moving
like a sleeper drugged with dreams
that will be forgotten by dawn.

Draco the Dragon is raising
his head above the horizon,
sweeping Polaris aside
with the slow swirl of his tail.

She watches as the heavens move
beyond her calculations,
precession pulling Polaris
out of her reach like cosmic wind
scattering the dust of stars.

SKIPPING STONES

It is somewhat like skipping stones
Across the river.

First you find a stone that knows your hand
With its weight and curve,
One solid and smooth and round.

Stance is important here;
An even base to ease the movement of the wrist,
The fingers curled just so.

It isn't a throwing motion you make
But more a holding back of hand and muscle
To balance the spin of your release.

You watch then,
Counting with breath held,
Measuring the distance and the speed.

With practice this becomes routine,
A gesture you make to amuse,
So many skims across the surface
That never disturb the liquid swell.

Sometimes though, you make a mistake.
The wrist weakens, the foot shifts
And the stone slices hard into the water,
Crying out in waves that lengthen from shore to shore.

SECRET WORK

The digital clock throbs out the seconds
Like a pulse heavy from exhaustion
Pushing blocks of blood through tunnels
Of arteries squeezing their way to the heart
Beating out its rhythm into the air that swirls
In and out of the spirals left by the
Figures moving through doors opening
Into rooms of nets thrown out to dry
After their secret work in the seas.

INVENTORY

One word is all you need to reconstruct
a chain of words linking out through memory

like a net to hold one face caught in one pose
that opens a moment of a season set against
other seasons you thought stored safely away
until one word drifts through the warehouse

and begins its small-fisted work inside
your eyes, inside your throat

SILENT SISTER

When we meet in the produce section
it takes you too long to recognize me, but
we recite the litany of jobs and lovers and addresses anyway
because we know it's expected of us, it's the required dance
people do after long separations.

We move through the aisles, agreeing
it is the best selection in the state;
kumquats, snow peas, tofu showcased
amid too many varieties of potatoes. We grew
up with routine choices, limp green beans,
hothouse tomatoes, suspect ears of corn.

You used to claim we were one another's skin
and I believed it. There was nothing we didn't tell
one another and it took years of talking before we
learned again the damage words can cause, so much
damage even our faithful silence betrayed us.

Now I offer you as much as I can
while pressing cellophaned produce, but you
remain as sealed as the freezers three aisles over.
I've had to give up everything
I couldn't live without. It's made my life so strong and
clean there is even space for you
again, room enough now for as many words
as you might want to say.

But you've given up nothing. I can see
how it's accumulated in your face, your eyes
so dazed with the hoarding
they've turned as dull as bruises.

We make our selections in silence.

I choose the heavy Idaho bakers and
you the bright swollen apples.
The stockboy begins rearranging pears
as I leave and start the careful counting
of things I should have said.

And you, safely home, you cleave
each piece of fruit you've bought
until your kitchen fills with perfect halves,
each one rocking silently on the counter.

-- *for lag*

FERRYMAN

You name your price
though it's only a litany,
a game you play just to hear
the pitch of their voices stiffen,
like the burdens they bring you.

Sometimes the survivors try to go
with you, pressing hard, offering
themselves like stones.

Between trips you imagine
different schemes, practice
escape routes in your mind
until they become as routine
as the lapping of water
against the bank, plans
as distant as the cold
etching the lines
of your face.

It is always dark.

You've long since sounded
the river, the current pulling
at your arms until they ache
like the slow ring of iron,

long since known the sound
is always your own voice calling
in the darkness, calling
at any price.

LIMESTONE

You wait for the bus on Limestone, stand
and watch the paper catch in the gutter,
watch the butts roll over and over in the street,
and you keep your eyes focused on a point
in front of you so they don't follow
every car that runs down the hill and slips
across the intersection and trails
its red tail lights behind it with a sound
like a hollow echo pulling out
the inside of your ears and if you knew
how to play the saxophone you would wail
the blues all the way up to the light that clicks
through its colors with routine fascination
as it sways a little in the wind,
would twist whatever coils inside you
into chords that would wash over the street
and sheet all the colors into a mist as fine as snow,
but being mute, you only pull your coat
a little closer and look down at your shoes,
waiting for the bus on Limestone.

TELL ME

What did you see
I want to know
if the faces appeared
in the rain
like warnings or like dreams
what did they say
to you as you stood
unsurprised on the sidewalk
(for hadn't you waited after all
your life for this)
was it a whisper like the sound
of one drop of rain acknowledged by the street
was it a human voice understanding
the pitch and frailty of the human ear
was it a question you had hoped
would be an answer
tell me
what did you reply
or were you struck dumb
face to face with the faces
you had so lovingly constructed
was there communion finally
some agreement reached
with relief like two lawyers
finally using the same words
how long did you stand there
the mist covering you
so that anyone interested enough
to notice would believe your face
ran with tears
would nod and move on
remembering their own tears
how long did it last
this encounter this materialization

and when it was finished
what then did you do
how long did you stand there
wordless the rain spreading
like speech across your skin
did you open your hands to touch
too late what you knew was gone
what most likely was never
there at all just an hallucination
something you imagined
like the unsaid sentences left
curled in your mouth
left like the lines
of your hands held out
to the empty spaces

GHOST

What love we gave holds
Its own shape now, a ghost wandering
About of its own accord calling
Out from the most unlikely places,
The spaces between
Notes of music, certain
glances between strangers.

I have long since moved
Beyond the usual
Sites of loss and pain, even desire
Is a place I no longer
Visit for those landmarks
I thought permanent
Have dissolved now into mist
As fine-grained as regret.

Yet still this ghost wanders hungry,
Patches of light already showing
Through its ribs. But I have no
Sustenance to offer,
No comfort left to give it.

OCTOBER

It is the same every October,
the same sudden cold, the same
wind stalking the frightened leaves
trapped against the same black trees.

Sometimes a chance tuning of the radio brings
one particular song and the sound remakes you
into who you were then and you know
if you turn you'll see
all of yourselves, aligned in a row
like ghosts, their separate lights tracking
through the distance.

Each one a distinct shape, each mouth
a blackness of words filling the air
with indecipherable sounds you've never understood,
never wanted to comprehend

for the ghost holding you now
might dissolve, might abandon you
without even a shadow
until you become as lost as the leaves
calling in their small secret voices.

So you stopped looking back several ghosts ago;
you just change the channel and make
another ghost at your back, watching
all the ones before you.

They shut down the fountains today
and the silence stretches across the city,
like the wind running its fingers through the trees,
searching for anything that might be left.

CHOCOLATE

They came in a cheap box,
thin plastic band posturing as ribbon,
cheap gold lettering on the brittle cover

that cracked with our first touch.
Chocolates from Belgium curved
into shell-etched creatures

swirled brown and white, caught
and waiting in their plastic beds,
waiting like sin waits

for that first turning.
Melted from the heat
of our hand, smeared

across the whorled tip of finger,
we took them slowly
like wine.

As thick and heavy with pleasure
as the secret we never spoke
but practiced all the same,

they spread over our tongue,
filling our mouth like comfort,
dark and whole.

PHASES OF THE MOON

You might want to know the phases of the moon for reasons
so personal you don't even tell yourself in those whispers
you mouth late in the night as your mind whirls to itself
dragging you through the weave of blackness that rips open
with your passing and hangs in ragged pieces that flutter
behind you as you move on through yet more blackness.

You may find it necessary to chart the movement of stars
as they arc like a knife slitting open a pattern where the
light bleeds through in silver narrowed by the distance into
points that transcribe themselves into words of a language
your brain has no way of translating into any tongue.

You might need a period of adjustment for the replacing of
bones in sockets loosened by the scream of elements as they
dance their way across your limbs that find no protection
against the wind that scatters the pattern and washes you
free of the things you believed to be the unchangeable
foundations of your existence until the only equation you
can trust is the circle opened out from the triangle born
of numbers woven of DNA where the slightest waver in the
cellular fluid will change your eyes brown and shift your
vision so you become blind to the familiar landmarks and
must feel your way with fingers of new nerves and muscle.

You may want to think of the time spent like snow that melts
into the fabric of your collar as you walk out into the cold
that freezes the center in your lungs and then turns white in
shapes that linger like the notes of bells from churches so
far away you'd never get near enough to walk through their
wooden doors and approach the altar where the sacraments are
no longer offered and even the wine has evaporated and turned
the air thick and dark like the dust in your pockets that
you pull out in handfuls and watch as it slips from your

fingers onto the floor making patterns of history you've read about in book but now look to you like the face you open to strangers.

EVENING MEAL

An old man and a young woman are having dinner
at the next table. She is, perhaps, his grown daughter.
She drinks her coffee with an abstract look in her eyes.
She is in a suit, and he wears a soft sweater,
with the shoulder seams drooping a little.
He carefully wipes his mouth
after every second bite, his napkin trembling.

There is a nursing home a few blocks south
and I think perhaps she has brought him out
for a forbidden meal. She does not watch him eat.

Perhaps she is wondering how much longer
he'll be able to feed himself,
how long before the cancer or the tumor or the madness,
already dangerously blooming, explodes
through his body. Perhaps she is thinking of asking someone
why these things happen, finding out what can be done.

He is thinking that he is proud of her,
that her mother would be proud of her,
that the dinner will surely cost more
than ten dollars, that ten dollars once paid
for a week's worth of groceries. He doesn't think
of his body, only that he must be careful
not to spill anything, not to embarrass her.

You understand I do not know these people,
that I am alone, trying only to have a quiet dinner.
It is the beginning of autumn. Occasionally the three of us
look out at the sky, at the colors stretched out
like banners over a deserted parade ground.

PERSPECTIVE

These days I'm like a newly healed man
who keeps forgetting he is whole,
waking up every morning with his vision
centered on the ceiling, still
believing his limbs lie paralyzed.

What bewilderment he feels
in those first moments he sees the room
bare of crutches and wheelchair, before
he remembers this is only another day
of relearning the habit of miracles.

Every morning he retests himself so carefully,
shaking away memory like a nightmare,
putting one foot and then the other on the solid
floor and standing up to see the world suddenly
righting itself into proper perspective.

These days I'm glad you're gone.

II

T.S. ELIOT IS DEAD

On Sundays when the seasons change
I get up early and make the coffee.
I open the windows and watch
the sun stretch, let the light fill
these rooms like the sound of the surf.

If I turn my head just so, I'll hear
the morning's first tourists walking
their dogs along the beach far off beyond
the skyline of houses where I can imagine
the ocean's endless searching across the sand,
between the rocks, as if whatever answer lies
land-locked could be released
with enough persistence. If it finds anything
worth knowing it carries it away.

I remember what you used to tell me,
how I used to believe it the way you believe
a nightmare might come true if you
accidentally cross the threshold during the day,
right foot first. I remember how hard I tried
to go through every door left foot first.
How impossible it is to never forget.

A bird calls past the window,
like a gull circling the cove.
Then I remember the ocean
works a thousand miles from here.

It rains here when the seasons change,
straight lines of it falling
like statements of irrefutable facts.
I have a reputation, I know

how things work, can name names
when it's necessary.

But Sundays are the hardest,
with the ocean a thousand miles way,
and the wrong foot on every threshold.

IRONWEEDS

Ironweeds in a vacant lot defying
the hard places of dry clay already
turning to dust and blowing in fine
half-hearted sheets for a few inches and
then spilling back to regain whatever strength
was lost in the crevices of cracked sidewalks
to be packed down by the steps of strangers
on their way past dark doorways held
open by the smell of decay left from worthless
furniture long since put out on the curb
and taken away by bulky figures in the early
morning riding the back of a truck that groans
under its burden of things no longer wanted
that will be shoveled in great piles
of earth turned over and over itself
like the restless sleep of some
creature tangled in the
night vines of the jungle

EVERY NIGHT

I call every night
Even though the phone is gone
And the ringing never reaches
Your empty room.

My fingers touch tones
Like a genetic code
Making a connection one-way.

And after awhile
I hang up, relieved
The silence still holds.

If you should answer
My heart would break again,
like cables snapping under
the weight of winter ice.

But I still call every night,
Thinking the signal might scatter,
Might reach you beyond the lines.

DUSK

The chill of winter
Seeping through the holes
Left behind by summer;

Leaves surrendering
Their claim to the sap
Of trees left speechless
By what their roots have
Sucked from the earth;

This street with its houses
Settled in rows like
Claims of immunity;

It is enough at dusk
To breath and wait,
Until skin, blood, and
Bone grow transparent to
The layers of the night.

ABSENCE

You are as distant now as the light
from one star caught in a chain of lights
spilled out onto wet avenues,
the palms of darkness pressed down
against glass streaked with reflected neon
where the cars pass slowly in a rain
slipping through its fingers.

GRAVITY

Newton said things want to move in a straight line,
Moving away at a sure and even pace.
He said once they began their journey
There would be a force to pull them back,
A force to hold as strong as the need to go.

Even the moon tries to pull away,
Circling like a ring pressing against a finger,
Pulling against the swollen joint of earth.
She tips herself in darkness,
Turns this way and that
Under the weight of light
Reshaping the planes of her face.

It isn't love that holds us together after all.
Moving against this need to escape,
This need to recapture, our lives
form curved lines arcing past one another
like planets caught between the sun and the dark.

FINAL CIRCLE

Having dusted off my sleeves,
having looked around once more in case
something's been left inadvertently behind,

having reached finality like a destination,
I remember it's all a circle,
over, endless, open,
repeated again and again
like some impossible length of film slipping
past the light that flashes the images in flickers
on my face,
on your face,
on whatever happens
to be in the way,

having worked out the Gordian knot of reason
until it lies flat and limp on the floor
I leave it for you to sweep away

or save,
curled in your hand and put aside
against the time you'll need to bind things
falling apart of their own nature.

FEEDER

The mind feeds on dark things,
Turning over the rotted soil
With cold fingers, always digging
Under the damp, always sifting through
Bits of objects broken and left
Behind, unrecognizable,
Half-buried, half-alive.

It goes on all night, this searching
Without aim under floodlights that
Arc over the crumpled ground in slow
Sweeps that thicken the darkness,

As the river stilled in its bed
Cuts deeper channels through its floor,
Seeking out faults weakened by the weight,
Searching for crevices that will open out
Beyond silt and rock into emptiness vast enough
To transmute the droplets into wind
That moves with certainty toward
A destination of clean structures built
With silence shaken free of the cold;

But there is only mantle,
Crusted into layers of hardness
Where one crack breaks into another,
Jolted steps that return again
And again to the same place;

And still the mind works on,
Eating handfuls of itself
Crouched with eyes glazed
And shoulders hunched, like
An animal gnawing its prey.

COUNTING

I count my unkindnesses like change
left at the end of the day, hoping
for fewer coins adding up to less.

I stack these regrets like dishes
I must eat from every day.

The faces of my mistakes talk at me
all night, in words I don't understand.

These things I've done
have carved their marks on my face,
lining out a map I must read each morning.

Every night the shape of this face
relives its deeds, the scars working
across my skin with numb fingers.

The moon remembers everything
And swells in silence, like grief.

WISHBONE

You have to pull it after dinner before the dishes are cleared away, take its thin edge in your fingers, close your eyes and sift through your mind for what state you'd like to be in forever and ever. You watch all the pictures of things you can have display themselves like contestants posing, one foot forward. You watch and wait for the one that's just right and when you decide you'll settle for that one there, you remember that all you ever really wanted was something honest and real and solid, the way old houses used to be built on the true, that maybe what you want is some light, some clarity illuminating whatever you put your hand to, some spark that puts everything into focus, into perspective, so you'll finally know the kind of freedom you imagine animals must possess, or maybe all you want is to be able to have one good cry like you used to when you were younger and misunderstood more than you do now, and then you pull, feeling the bone's hardened calcium holding onto itself for dear life

THEY WILL TELL LIES AT YOUR FUNERAL

They will stand beside the dirt
while the wind gathers the leaves like bones
and take your silence for assent
to straighten themselves, to turn
their clever attention to stories you had no part in.
They will polish your character like a coin
in the sun to blind us with your goodness,
your charitable acts, your courage.

You were a coward most of your days,
fear winding about you
like a snake, its poison turning
everything to pain until you became
as crippled as the cat at your door that kept
crying, no matter what you fed it.

You grew so afraid you would not speak,
just let the words blossom inward
and turn you into a thing of thorns
holding off the world the distance of torn skin.

They tell me it is customary to enhance the dead,
to make them more than they were in life,
as if the living is never enough.

Why should you care how many lies they tell?
You are as free now as the lily of the valley overtaking
the lawn, and the voice of your memory
calls like rose petals pushing outward.

TURNING

Maybe it's true
that endings are beginnings,
but your face doesn't look as if
it were turned toward something new.
I keep noticing that my hands are not opened
to the future.

It's so hard to remember that our separate lives
have been moving all along to bring us together,
that even tonight they're moving us toward others
we can't imagine ever wanting.

We should just smile and promise
that we'll remember, knowing we don't know
what we'll remember at all, knowing instead
that in two months or seven years
it will be a stray scent or the way a stranger
moves their wrist that brings everything back.

We will turn then, amazed
at how far we've come, how far apart
we've moved, how close we came.

BODIES

Are you there?
Can you hear me?
I've been learning all this time how to say things plain,
trying to follow this thin line you've left me.

No one has forgotten you. I still find flowers
left by strangers, even in the dead of winter.

All that last morning you kept turning
from the nurses and doctors, fighting
not death this time, but only to be left alone,
spared the final proofs of your body's betrayal.

That night a friend came to the house to tell me
how other people handle the mechanics of death,
how to deal with obituaries and neighbors, exactly
what I would be feeling at any point in the weeks ahead.
I felt nothing. Only a floating, everything in sharp relief,
like the sudden realization the lawn needed cutting again.
I picked out your clothes automatically; the handmade dress,
the slip you always said was too good to wear. Long past
midnight I floated on my bed like a stranger, pressing
your sweater to me, your smell the only thing holding me
through the long hours of blackness.

All I felt at your funeral was relief that never again
would you awaken at three in the morning
screaming for people dead sixty years, never look at me
with such hatred and demand to know who I was,
that I would never have to go into your kitchen again
and cook as if I were the adult and you were the child.
Love was never a factor in our battles, only hatred
of the helpless crumbling of your mind.

I learned my body would never swell enough to hold
my grief, that it would be years before grief
was finished carving its design into my body.

Genetics have given me your bones, your skin and hair,
the same immunities and frailties, my body follows
the same journey your body made.

When I have to fight now I never remember
where I learned such courage, only feel it burn in me
as nameless and familiar as my breath.

Can you hear me?
My breath, your breath,
they both go on.

—for ldkf

SALT

It is best, after all,
to turn your face for one more look
for you know it must last;
know you must let it burn into your blood
so deeply its memory will encode itself
into the blood of your unborn children.

What good is the turning away
when the future has no face,
no voice to comfort the ear?
What use is a destination
when the only clarity is what you must leave?

It is best, after all, to become
the pillar of salt in the desert
rather than to be cut so by such loss
that you become two people walking
side by side down the same road;
best to let the wind eat at your face
until you blur into one smooth shape,
your ear holding the call of your name
from a far distance, your voice
stricken mute amid so much sand.

SAYING GOOD-BYE

I never say it right. Always the syntax
gets twisted, my mind won't supply
the necessary adjectives, so that we end
up looking at one another like strangers
on the street. You'd think one of us was asking
for money, the way we stare at each other.

The problem is that I'm seeing
the future, am already preparing
myself to be that person over there,
the one whose life does not include him.
She wants him to take away his hand
because she knows how often she'll remember it,
how her skin will remind her of its absence
in the months to come. He knows
when he stops touching her he'll vanish,
slowly, like the process of evaporation.

How can anyone be clear with all these details
pressing at them?

Someone should write a book, citing
the proper method of parting, explaining
what there is to hold onto in that moment
the world splits open and we're both left
standing, empty-handed, on the sidewalk.

BEGETTING

I know who you love.
I've watched you watch
faces turning in crowds
whenever they believed
they were alone.

I see you watching,
changing your face,
your absorption smoothing
its fingers across your
features so that I see you
becoming who you love.

It is a long chain
of master linking
master, the past
nodding to the present
dreaming the future
as it learns the watching.

Already the bones of my face
are softening like clay
from my watching
so that what I see in the mirror
is the stranger I was
meant to become.

There should be
an exponential progression
to all this; one begetting two,
two begetting four, four eight, until
everyone is chosen.
But there never is.

One begets only one,
watching and memorizing,
learning what is loved, what is left
behind, seeing who is chosen,
who is passed over.

MECHANICS

She sits alone in the lit room,
head bent over book. Occasionally
she moves her hand to make a note, learning
the mechanics of remembering.

In the rooms above and below her
the janitors walk past the windows,
the sunlight striping their faces
like streaks of paint.

I am in the next building. All day
I watch the students fill and empty
the room with great slowness,
like a surrealistic wave
trapped in a Plexiglas cube.

She is waiting. I can see
how she looks up just before
the door opens and the teacher
comes in. He nods as if they
might be strangers. He moves
to the window and snaps closed
the blinds, like eyelids quickly
shutting out too much light.

And the light pulls away, startled
at such abandonment. Everywhere
there is something to fear.

WIDOW WALK

After awhile the eye demands that you turn and leave, not because you no longer care, never that, but simply because the eye is a selfish organ and insists on variety. It will tear as you stare out at the endless waters so that anyone seeing you might believe you surrendering to grief when in fact it is only the eye's boredom. You have moved beyond grief, your face finally set into its final lines as you've considered every possible and impossible situation and solution and still arrived at nothing but silence. Whatever prayers you once offered return to you like small birds fluttering as you turn for home, remembering that a bird in a house portends death. If you were a Buddhist you would loosen the absence in the house and let it dissolve like fine-grained salt in water, could turn to your work with the protection of indifference as if you were safely someone else.

But you are no one else now, barely able to own your own face, knowing already what loneliness will do to you, how it will carve itself into your face, press against your back until you bend slightly forward under its weight as you walk through the town in the long summer afternoons, the little children stopping to stare.

THE USUAL STORY

It's the usual story, two people who want to be together, but can't because all along they thought they were doing the right thing, but later found out they weren't, and now they both have to just make do with what they have, and what they have now doesn't ever quite fit right again, like a dress in the closet you thought perfectly suitable before you woke up last week and realized you'd gained weight and the dress seems to have shrunk all along the seams and just doesn't flatter you the way it did last summer at the cookout where you drank frozen daiquiris all afternoon and made clever conversation with your husband's boss who later said he hadn't realized how intelligent and perceptive you were, while you secretly thought what a bore he was to be so engrossed in what to you was so obvious, if only he had enough sense to read a newspaper once in a while, but then you remember you've always liked being slightly out of step in this neighborhood, that if you really tried you too could learn the pleasure of making an outing to the latest mall, breathing in the conditioned air and listening to the piped-in music that sounds suspiciously like an old Eagles' song you used to play over and over on your stereo, with the headphones on, years ago when you believed in the things songs used to be about, but of course, we're all adults here and we know there's no point in complaining about what can't be changed, despite all those self-help books you used to buy before you went back to college and had to declare a major, for once forced into telling the world what you thought of yourself, what you valued above all else, and how you worried, late at night, what people would say to you once they knew, but of course, no one said anything, as if your life was something that had been decided beyond you for years, and even now you're not convinced it was enough, that if you'd tried a little harder, took a few more risks, but you're imagining again that things could be different from what they are, that decisions made could be undone like a knot being untied, that any life would be better than this, that any story could be told better by anyone but you.

III

LINES

after your eyes have adjusted
to the differences between light and dark
and you have gained some amount of confidence
in how to move about

you find a line

broad and sharp and clear and there's no mistaking
that this is a boundary and even though no one has given
you a passport you slide one foot over that line
thinking you'll be safe
you find another place, another land with new shapes
of light and dark and make no mistake
you get so scared your veins turn to ice and harden
until your body threatens to burst
into a shattering of sound and light

until you realize the cold was only
that odd neural response to heat
and you turn in the warmth and grow
and open like one of those impossible blossoms
in the botanical gardens of the rich

and after you've adjusted once more to light and dark

you find a line

PATTERN

The pattern is as intricate
as any tapestry woven
by one Celtic woman waiting
for the battle to end,
her hands pulling the threads
into mazes of colors and figures
of unicorns and dazed-faced knights,
lacking perspective as the scenes lengthen
across the frame until they unfurl to the floor,
where the dogs lie quiet and watch.

QUILTS

One simple remnant with its own texture and style,
Reminding you of things you've seen, moments you've had.
So you put it away, saving against another time.

After bits of months knitted into years
Other pieces appear until one afternoon
You open a drawer and find heaps
Of little stacks taking too much room.

You make your quilt then,
Cutting the pieces to fit a pattern
Someone once told you about, stitching
Colors and weaves, smoothing layers
Together from the center outward.

And when it's done, finished
In your own design, you can fold
Its thickness and put it away. Or unfurl
It over your bed, assurance against any cold.

THIS HOUSE

I've never known this house to be so quiet.
These rooms swallow like an open mouth
Any protests I might have made,
Eating sounds like words mouthed
Under water, pressed down
By their own weight until turned
Inside outward the currents
Pull the syllables into shreds
That rise to the surface and float
Like bits of litter no one will clear away
For the sea always takes care of its own.

This house mocks me with echoes
Of answers I have no use for,
Like snapshots sent to the blind.
I finger the edges for Braille,
And finding no message let them fall
Where they settle about my feet
And reform the shape of my steps
I leave behind as I move
From place to place.

This house once coiled about me
Like an elastic band certain
Of its grip now grown slack
From too many bundles too strong
And too large to be held
Until what had been contained scatters
Like birds in a winter field
Where the snow grown weary of whispers
Lies silent sifting itself into ice.

COLD COUNTRY

When the day has died with the sound of
Empty museums in late afternoons where
You've gone to fit the fragments between
Hours together in patterns that will hold
But then come to look to you like pieces
Of meteorites flung to the earth by
Forces that were dispersed into the cold
Country of the stars long before you thought
To creep out of the waters and shake loose
The bits of sodden green still clinging
To your skin and force your muscles
Into new tensions against the slanted
Gravity of a curved world;

The weight lies heavy in your hands,
Numbing your fingers until finally
You let it fall onto the ground
Where it rolls for a distance
Over the grass and then stops.

And you look at it for a while,
Wiping your palms against your thighs,
Wondering how long it will hold your eyes,
How long before your feet send out tendrils
Into the ground, feeling their way
So deep into the earth your skin
Begins to harden like bark and the wind
Becomes a rustling sound in your ears.

BRILLIANCE

From the beginning your mind whirled and spun
in a dizzying weave of sound and color and you
followed it willingly, as if that's what people do.
You let it run as easily as sunlight, your face brilliant
with the things it showed you.

No one told you where this process would take you.
How could they? They just kept a safe distance and held
their breath, stood back and let you go on, only half listening
to the intricate language you found necessary to describe everything.

When you saw just how little was understood, realized you were
alone, you learned to repeat yourself. Often you spoke slowly,
puzzling over which was needed more, the repeating or the sharing.

You began to think you were caught in some trick of light,
like a common carnival act everyone knows so well they need
never mention it. You wasted years learning there was no
way out of the illusionist's mirrors, wasted even more time
learning no MC's cry would ever widen enough to hold you.

At night the colors and lights still sing, your mind twisting
as it goes about its secret work. You stand in your dreams
like a stranger, watching with someone else's face.
And in the long light of mornings you begin again
the slow process of translation, repeating
the words so no one misunderstands.

FOR A PIANO PLAYER

You'll play for anyone these days,
Hands translating any request,
Your selection process worn down
By the endless random tunings
All channels stay open now,
Letting in sound and static alike.

Your ear long lost to that
Mathematical tangle of chords,
Your eyes never see the singer
Moved to words at your shoulder
Or the dancers sliding their steps
In perfect rhythm to your tempo.

Your structures are the liquids
Of sound and your bones
Have dissolved until you flow
Like vibrato in answer to scales
Spilled out in bars that line
The skin of your fingered palms.

It's no difference to you anymore
What you play when or where.
All you want is the question
That will open your hands and
Move them, like a swimmer,
Parting the waters for breath.

CHAMELEON

They come into your life like
Bits of foam churned out by
The waves of the ocean beyond
The shores where you wait.

They float through your days like
Petals from colored flowers and you
Chameleon fade from one to another.

They go out of your life like
Lone birds joined in high patterns
Clutching shares of your flesh
As they fly beyond your vision.

TOURIST

You watch the waves suspiciously;
it is perhaps the only time you face
something inattentive of your voice,
something stronger than yourself.

Already you are breaking
like ice in water, the pieces
floating farther apart.

I want to take more pictures,
but I know it is too late
in the season for clarity;
your face is as gray
as the light, as intent
as the gulls searching for
a thin line of horizon.

In the motel we watch Wheel of Fortune,
outguessing everyone. If we
had been on the air
we would be rich by now.

Nearly a year later the pictures
reveal little of that day;

only the monotonous stretch
of sea, only the slight, last
indecision as you turn, frowning
into the sinking sun.

SUNFLOWERS

You came, you said, to tell me what you had made
of the time in between, those long years of absence
brushed aside like dust. Above all else, you said, it was
the sunflowers you most wanted me to see now. How tall
they stood, as if holding up the small building
beside your house, how straight they rose to the sun.

I remembered the small white building beside the house,
the afternoon we sorted through papers and accumulated
mementos of other lives, how easily you moved past
the broken chairs and stacks of ragged magazines, like
someone who belonged there.

You sat in my kitchen, explaining the importance
of learning to grow, learning to move with the seasons.
We were listening to new age music, an endless ribbon of
piano that kept pulling at me like taffy while your voice
made its familiar slow circling dance. It was spring,
the sky dark and shaken with thunder.

The stalks, you said, grow so strong that you use them
as stakes for next season's tomatoes. I could see the tiny bits
of colored cloth fluttering in a sudden afternoon wind, see
the clean lines of your fingers as you tied fast each strip.

The blossoms grow larger than your head, you said. Sometimes
you sit on the back deck and watch birds pull at the seeds, watch
the flowers bend ever so slightly and then let go.
You give everything away in the fall, you said.
Why save anything?

Now I think only of the necessary horror, the wet earth,
the fracturing of each seed, the struggle in the darkness.

No wonder they grow so straight, climbing
as far from the ground as they can reach, turning
their wide faces to sun and rain, opening
themselves to whatever breed of bird chances by.

—*for drg*

BRIDGES

You stand on the bank
In the dusk watching
The transparent flames
Flutter through the wood
Until the darkness turns
Them golden against the ash
And the moon looks up at you
From the water and you bind
It to silence as you wait
Watching the fire feed
Until the planks begin to fall

HALLWAYS

Last night I heard the janitor singing. He was singing about Italy, about the fountains of Rome and a woman with bare arms as white as the moon. Maybe it was love, maybe it was indifference, maybe he knew the difference. He sang absently as if it wouldn't make the time go faster but might make the time more interesting. Her name was Rosalee, and I wondered why it wasn't Maria, but maybe she came from Spanish blood and that's why he loved her, all that dark Spanish blood making dove-white skin. Perhaps she is old now, stooped a little, certainly pot-bellied from the fifteen children she bore Alberto who was too fond of the wine and the dances and died in 1974 of heart failure, but then, don't we all?

The janitor sings this song every night, the hallways glistening behind him like white arms in moonlight.

FOURTH OF JULY RUN

They cordon off the streets
Early, before the city begins to stir
And move itself in cars. The police
Wear fluorescent vests and move

Their fingers across maps
While they drink coffee and remember
How many sawhorses, how many
Orange cones wait in the vans.

The vendors pull in and begin
Unloading their tired trucks, assembling
Stands and cursing the one piece
That never fits

Without a fight. Members
Of the bands straighten
Their coats as the stray note
Of a french horn catches

On the glint of a baton practicing
Its freefall through the air. While
The MC and his friends settle
In the grandstand and the sun

Pulls away the mist with its climb,
The runners gather and stretch
Their multicolored limbs
Like dancers at the barre.

They eye the fluttering banner
Marking out the starting place
And dream they lift their arms
To feel the final ribbon break.

When the official consults his watch
The runners tense as one,
Until the crack of the track gun
Startles them, sudden

birds flocking south.

CRESCENT MOON

Tonight the crescent moon hangs as thin and sharp
as the nail of a woman who's been thinking
all night, looking at the moon, holding herself
like a forgotten gift. When she goes
to the bureau for the pistol, her mind is as clear
as the air, light as the thin coat of oil
on the metal. It lies
in her palm as heavy as sin. How easily
she moves to the door, as if
she were a character in a movie, gliding
silently across a marble floor.

Every night the moon goes through this, holding
itself carefully, as if its light might break
the sky like ice.

YOGA

Feel how cleanly the large thigh muscle allows itself to be pulled, stretched slowly to its farthest reach. Put both arms out before you, hands together, and bend forward into yourself until your hands rest on the fragile ankle. Be aware of your spine giving up its hold to allow each vertebrae its own space in which to curl so that your entire body becomes a smooth rounded thing of tension relaxed. Hold this position until you understand the stillness in your mind.

Lift your arms to point to the source of light flooding the sky, each tendon supporting the weight of bone and pump of blood, the spine this time an imaginary line connecting the seven chakras.

Repeat this exercise three times.

When you have finished, rise to your natural height. Fill your lungs with air and walk away.

WITNESS

when they urge him to take expression to its fullest limits
it isn't him they're thinking of, but themselves
it's a comfort to watch someone else
run screaming through the streets, stop suddenly
and grab their hair and pull as if by sheer force
the brain could be straightened into controllable circuits
of thought and thus translated to the heart
it's the same principle as accidents on the street
that twisted fascination of someone else's cries
before the ambulance finally arrives to clear the area
we're so pleased it isn't us we don't notice the guilt
leading us carefully to the sadness that it has to be anyone
we wonder if that's what we would do lying in their place
if that's what our pain would sound like in the thin cold air
and how no one else would cry for us in that exact pitch

HIGH DIVE

You stop right at the edge of the board, your toes taking
in the sharp edge. You stop and breathe, let your heart
measure out its beating. All around you
is the clear blue of sky, the glass of water beckoning.

You know how it will feel, all that water opening
for you, letting your body arc like a strange beautiful
animal gliding silver amid blue.

Inside there is always a moment
before you open your eyes, suspended beyond
gravity and desire, when you consider
remaining in the darkness of yourself,
weigh the advantages of never
returning to the surface.

But then your wrists and palms curve upward
as if in prayer, leading your body back to break
through the surface, to the surprising air
cutting clean into your lungs.

ROAD WORK

The first thing you do is get in.
Your license and the manual
won't help you here.
Throw them out.

Start the engine
and let its life move
you out onto the road,
along with everyone else.

The first intersection
will be familiar, one
you've turned into so often
you know its angle by heart.
Pass it by.

It will be a long journey,
the span of a swollen second
pulling the mountains into
bridges arcing themselves
from one state to another.

Speed will take its own shape,
make its own hand to hold
you safe against the blaze of lights
rushing outside the window.

Continue in a straight line
even as the traffic thins.
The earth will crack open then,
yawn in a terrible fissure.
This need not concern you.

Your zen indifference will lift you,
move you in a smooth line upward.
Let the landscapes retreat back
to your imagination where,
you realize, they've been all along.

I DON'T CARE

When I say I don't care it doesn't mean that I don't care exactly, although in some cases it means just that. It's just that there are degrees of indifference. Take the place where I work, for example. Everyone there is twisted somehow. Some of them express this physically, like a permanently pulled muscle in their back that forces them to walk with the slightest irregularity. Some of them cry periodically, usually the middle-management women who keep wads of tissues in their suitcoat pockets and refuse to paint their nails any more because they obsessively peel off the layers of mauve or red or hint of coral. Maybe they believe that by removing the temptation they'll stop the urge, though I've found just the opposite is true.

None of us speak well. When forced into the verbal arena we sputter like a worn out engine, lose the subject of the sentence immediately and spend long agonizing minutes trying to chase it down.

It isn't that I don't care. I will argue this point all day, the distinctions between not caring at all and not caring any more and caring so much I understand the necessity of standing apart, like one of the guys at the airport with the florescent wands in his hands who recognizes our need for signals but understands even more the importance of keeping clear.

EVERYONE'S DAUGHTER

Having duly noted that I've passed
every test they could offer, they've
decided to let me in. It's official now,
this bargain we've made.

Someone very thoughtful has taken
me by the hand and is carefully
explaining what things mean.
I know what things mean.

I was here once before
but all the doors were closed
and the windows dark. The butler
said I'd have to come back.

So I went somewhere else
and tried to forget this was the place
I wanted to be. But sometimes
you know where you belong
and nothing will erase it.

They're all around me now,
these strangers with their kind faces
turning to me like a parade
of portraits in the great hall.

I could be everyone's daughter,
standing here while someone takes
away the baggage and tips the driver.

They can make of me
whatever they like,
my face goes with anything.
But I'm my own daughter now
and I know who we are.

CROSSING THE DIVIDE

Already the snow is beginning, the headlights turning it into
sticks of white, thousands of them, all pointed and moving
toward your face faster than you can drive at three in the
morning just before the interstate narrows into that long
torturous stretch pulling across the mountains and you
understand that whatever happens now will be a sign
you were wrong about everything, or right.

It is so dark you can't see the falling away of the summit beside
you but you know it's there, feel the emptiness calling you back
like protection,

and still you climb, signs appearing in the darkness like sudden
lights, signs marking elevations with numbers that mean nothing
to you, signs offering cautions in that secret language of grades
and gear down and runaway ramps, as if trucks were mute beasts
with no words but what they came seeking on the faces of signs.

From the west a few semis come toward you like people you see
in the street who won't meet your eyes, as if you've missed again
what was important, and still the meeting of rubber against
asphalt holds you to every curve as you meet each point of
darkness, pass through and on to the next, and it isn't fear you
feel anymore, that's all turned now into resignation

and finally there is one small sign marking out the eastern
continental divide in white capital letters, announcing your
passage back into the place you thought you could escape, so
you think about that place, about the lights lining its streets in
the night rain, hear again the great rushing of the rivers releasing
from the locks, think of the early sun spreading through the sky
like peace caught on fire, how the Indians called it kaintuck, the
dark and bloody ground and you know it's so even in the sound

of the mountains' slow dark song, and you think then of the men
and remember one turning the darkness of coal into the light of
steel, how you've tasted the colors of it in his skin,

how your native place is a hand and you were born at the wrist
where the Ohio moves like the body's blood, how you live now
in the palm of that hand where you've seen the thoroughbreds
run in snow, and you remember all the years you've spent
beyond the upcurled fingers of the Appalachians, and you don't
know how such a dark and bloody place can sing with such life
and motion, but it does,

sometimes so clearly the vibrato rings the moon with light, and
when the road suddenly releases you back to the comfort of the
interstate, the sky begins to open with light and you feel the faces
of all the people you've ever been and all the people you're
becoming gathering in your face, gathering themselves in your
own dark blood, and singing,

singing to be finally getting home again.

Marguerite Floyd holds an MFA from Vermont College of Fine Arts. Her poetry and non-fiction have appeared nationally and internationally. She makes her home in central Kentucky.

www.ingramcontent.com/pod-product-compliance
Lightning Source LLC
Chambersburg PA
CBHW031207090426
42736CB00009B/821
* 9 7 8 1 8 9 3 2 3 9 9 1 3 *